THE NEW DEAL IN HISTORICAL PERSPECTIVE

By FRANK FREIDEL

Harvard University

SERVICE CENTER FOR TEACHERS OF HISTORY

A Service of the American Historical Association

400 A Street, S. E. Washington, D. C. 20003

Library of Congress catalog card number: 59–15910

Composed and Printed at Waverly Press, Inc.
Baltimore, Maryland 21202

Printed in the United States of America

COMMITTEE ON TEACHING OF THE

AMERICAN HISTORICAL ASSOCIATION

THE NEW DEAL IN HISTORICAL PERSPECTIVE

Frank Freidel

In less than a generation, the New Deal has passed into both popular legend and serious history. The exigencies of American politics long demanded that its partisans and opponents paint a picture of it either in the most glamorous whites or sinister blacks. Long after the New Deal was over, politicians of both major parties tried at each election to reap a harvest of votes from its issues.

Gradually a new generation of voters has risen which does not remember the New Deal and takes for granted the changes that it wrought. Gradually too, politicians have had to recognize that the nation faces new, quite different problems since the second World War, and that campaigning on the New Deal has become as outmoded as did the "bloody shirt" issue as decades passed after the Civil War. At the same time, most of the important manuscript collections relating to the New Deal have been opened to scholars so rapidly that careful historical research has been possible decades sooner than was true for earlier periods of United States history. (The Franklin D. Roosevelt papers and the Abraham Lincoln papers became available for research at about the same time, just after the second World War.)

It has been the task of the historians not only to analyze heretofore hidden aspects of the New Deal on the basis of the manuscripts, but also to remind readers of what was once commonplace and is now widely forgotten. A new generation has no firsthand experience of the depths of despair into which the depression had thrust the nation, and the excitement and eagerness with which people greeted the new program. Critics not only have denied that anything constructive could have come from the New Deal but they have even succeeded in creating the impression in the prosperous years since 1945 that the depression really did not amount to much. How bad it was is worth remembering, since this is a means of gauging the enormous pressure for change. Estimates of the number of unemployed ranged up to thirteen

1

million out of a labor force of fifty-two million, which would mean that one wage-earner out of four was without means of support for himself or his family. Yet of these thirteen million unemployed, only about a quarter were receiving any kind of assistance. States and municipalities were running out of relief funds; private agencies were long since at the end of their resources. And those who were receiving aid often obtained only a pittance. The Toledo commissary could allow for relief only 2.14 cents per person per meal, and the Red Cross in southern Illinois in 1931 was able to provide families with only seventy-five cents a week for food. It was in this crisis that one of the most flamboyant members of the Hoover administration suggested a means of providing sustenance for the unemployed: restaurants should dump left-overs and plate scrapings into special sanitary cans to be given to worthy un-employed people willing to work for the food. It was a superfluous suggestion, for in 1932 an observer in Chicago reported:

> Around the truck which was unloading garbage and other refuse were about thirty-five men, women, and children. As soon as the truck pulled away from the pile, all of them started digging with sticks, some with their hands, grabbing bits of food and vegetables.

The employed in some instances were not a great deal better off. In December 1932 wages in a wide range of industries from textiles to iron and steel, averaged from a low of 20 cents to a high of only 30 cents an hour. A quarter of the women working in Chicago were receiving less than 10 cents an hour. In farming areas, conditions were equally grim. In bitter weather on the Great Plains, travelers occasionally encountered a light blue haze that smelled like roasting coffee. The "old corn" held over from the crop of a year earlier would sell for only $1.40 per ton, while coal cost $4 per ton, so many farmers burned corn to keep warm. When Aubrey Williams went into farm cellars in the Dakotas in the early spring of 1933 farm wives showed him shelves and shelves of jars for fruits and vegetables—but they were all empty. Even farmers who could avoid hunger had trouble meeting payments on their mortgages. As a result a fourth of all farmers in the United States lost their farms during these years.

Despairing people in these pre-New Deal years feared President Herbert Hoover had forgotten them or did not recognize the seriousness of their plight. As a matter of fact he had, more than any other depression president in American history, taken steps to try to bring recovery. But he had functioned largely through giving aid at the top to prevent the further collapse of banks and industries, and the concentric rings of further collapses and unemployment which would then ensue. Also he had continued to pin his faith upon voluntary action. He felt that too great federal intervention would undermine the self-reliance, destroy the "rugged individualism" of the American people, and that it would create federal centralization, thus paving the way for socialism.

President Hoover was consistent in his thinking, and he was humane. But it would have been hard to explain to people like those grubbing on the Chicago garbage heap, why, when the Reconstruction Finance Corporation was loaning $90,000,000 to a single Chicago bank, the President would veto a bill to provide federal relief for the unemployed, asserting, "never before has so dangerous a suggestion been seriously made in this country." It was not until June 1932 that he approved a measure permitting the RFC to loan $300,000,000 for relief purposes.

It seems shocking in retrospect that such conditions should have existed in this country, and that any president of either major party should so long have refused to approve federal funds to alleviate them. It adds to the shock when one notes that many public figures of the period were well to the right of the President—for instance, Secretary of the Treasury Andrew Mellon—and that almost no one who was likely to be in a position to act, including Governor Roosevelt of New York, was ready at that time to go very far to the left of Hoover.

Roosevelt, who was perhaps the most advanced of the forty-eight governors in developing a program to meet the depression, had shown little faith in public works spending. When he had established the first state relief agency in the United States in the fall of 1931, he had tried to finance it through higher taxes, and only later, reluctantly, abandoned the pay-as-you-go basis. He was, and he always remained, a staunch believer in a balanced budget. He was never more sincere than when, during the campaign of 1932, he accused the Hoover administration of having run up a deficit of three and three-quarters billions of dollars in the previous two years. This, he charged, was "the most reckless and extravagant past that I have been able to discover in the statistical record of any peacetime Government anywhere, any time."

Governor Roosevelt's own cautious record did not exempt him from attack. In April 1932, seeking the presidential nomination, he proclaimed himself the champion of the "forgotten man," and talked vaguely about raising the purchasing power of the masses, in part through directing Reconstruction Finance Corporation loans their way. This little was sufficient to lead many political leaders and publicists, including his Democratic rival, Al Smith, to accuse Roosevelt of being a demagogue, ready to set class against class.

Smith and most other public figures, including Roosevelt, favored public works programs. A few men like Senators Robert F. Wagner of New York and Robert M. La Follette of Wisconsin visualized really large-scale spending on public construction, but most leaders also wanted to accompany the spending with very high taxes which would have been deflationary and thus have defeated the program. None of the important political leaders, and none of the economists who had access to them, seemed as yet to visualize the decisive intervention of the government into the economy of the sort that is considered commonplace today. The term "built-in stabilizers" had yet to be coined.

The fact was that Roosevelt and most of his contemporaries, who like him were products of the Progressive Era, were basically conservative men who unquestioningly believed in the American free enterprise system. On the whole, they were suspicious of strong government, and would indulge in it only as a last resort to try to save the system. This was their limitation in trying to bring about economic recovery. On the other hand, part of their Progressive legacy was also a humanitarian belief in social justice. This belief would lead them to espouse reforms to improve the lot of the common man, even though those reforms might also take them in the direction of additional government regulation. Roosevelt as governor had repeatedly demonstrated this inconsistency in his public statements and recommendations. He had ardently endorsed states rights and small government in a truly Jeffersonian way. Then in quite contrary fashion (but still in keeping with

Jeffersonian spirit applied to twentieth century society) he had pointed out one or another area, such as old age security, in which he believed the government must intervene to protect the individual.

At this time, what distinguished Governor Roosevelt from his fellows were two remarkable characteristics. The first was his brilliant political skill, which won to him an overwhelming proportion of the Democratic politicians and the general public. The second was his willingness to experiment, to try one or another improvisation to stop the slow economic drift downward toward ruin. During the campaign of 1932, many a man who had observed Roosevelt felt as did Harry Hopkins that he would make a better president than Hoover, "chiefly because he is not afraid of a new idea."

Roosevelt's sublime self-confidence and his willingness to try new expedients stood him in good stead when he took over the presidency. On that grim March day in 1933 when he took his oath of office, the American economic system was half-paralyzed. Many of the banks were closed; the remainder he quickly shut down through presidential proclamation. Industrial production was down to 56 per cent of the 1923–25 level. Yet somehow, Roosevelt's self-confidence was infectious. People were ready to believe, to follow, when he said in words that were not particularly new, "The only thing we have to fear is fear itself." He offered "leadership of frankness and vigor," and almost the whole of the American public and press—even papers like the Chicago *Tribune* which soon became bitter critics—for the moment accepted that leadership with enthusiasm.

For a short period of time, about one hundred days, Roosevelt had behind him such overwhelming public support that he was able to push through Congress a wide array of legislation which in total established the New Deal. It came in helter-skelter fashion and seemed to go in all directions, even at times directions that conflicted with each other. There was mildly corrective legislation to get the banks open again, a slashing of government costs to balance the budget, legalization of 3.2 beer, establishment of the Civilian Conservation Corps, of the Tennessee Valley Authority, and of a wide variety of other agencies in the areas of relief, reform, and, above all in those first months, of recovery.

What pattern emerged in all of this legislation? How sharply did it break with earlier American political traditions? The answer was that it represented Roosevelt's efforts to be president to all the American people, to present something to every group in need. And it was based squarely on American objectives and experience in the Progressive Era and during the first World War. It went beyond the Hoover program in that while the word "voluntary" remained in many of the laws, they now had behind them the force of the government or at least strong economic incentives.

It has been forgotten how basically conservative Roosevelt's attitudes remained during the early period of the New Deal. He had closed the banks, but reopened them with relatively little change. Indeed, the emergency banking measure had been drafted by Hoover's Treasury officials. What banking reform there was came later. His slashing of the regular government costs was something he had promised during his campaign, and in which he sincerely believed and continued to believe. He kept the regular budget of the government low until the late thirties. While he spent billions through the parallel emergency budget, he did that reluctantly, and only because he felt it was necessary to keep people from starving. He was proud that he was keeping the credit of the government good, and never ceased to look forward to the day when he could balance the budget. For the first several years of the New Deal he consulted frequently with Wall Streeters and other economic conservatives. His first Director of the Budget, Lewis Douglas, parted ways with him, but late in 1934 was exhorting: "I hope, and hope most fervently, that you will evidence a real determination to bring the budget into actual balance, for upon this, I think, hangs not only your place in history but conceivably the immediate fate of western civilization." (Douglas to FDR, November 28, 1934)

Remarks like this struck home with Roosevelt. Douglas's successors as Director of the Budget held much the same views, and Henry Morgenthau, Jr., who became Secretary of the Treasury at the beginning of 1934, never failed to prod Roosevelt to slash governmental expenditures.

We should add parenthetically that Roosevelt always keenly re-

sented the untrue newspaper stories that his parents had been un-
willing to entrust him with money. As a matter of fact he was
personally so thrifty when he was in the White House that he used
to send away for bargain mail-order shirts, and when he wished
summer suits, switched from an expensive New York tailor to a
cheaper one in Washington. This he did despite the warning of
the New York tailor that he might thus lose his standing as one of
the nation's best-dressed men.

Financial caution in governmental affairs rather typifies Roosevelt's economic thinking throughout the entire New Deal. He was
ready to go much further than Hoover in construction of public
works, but he preferred the kind which would pay for themselves,
and did not think there were many possibilities for them in the
country. His estimate before he became president was only one
billion dollars worth. In 1934, he once proposed that the government buy the buildings of foundered banks throughout the nation
and use them for post-offices rather than to construct new buildings. This is how far he was from visualizing huge public works
expenditures as a means of boosting the country out of the depression. His course in this area was the middle road. He wished to
bring about recovery without upsetting the budget any further
than absolutely necessary. He did not launch the nation on a
program of deliberate deficit financing.

When Roosevelt explained his program in a fireside chat at the
end of July 1933, he declared:

"It may seem inconsistent for a government to cut down its
regular expenses and at the same time to borrow and to spend
billions for an emergency. But it is not inconsistent because a large
portion of the emergency money has been paid out in the form of
sound loans...; and to cover the rest...we have imposed
taxes....

"So you will see that we have kept our credit good. We have
built a granite foundation in a period of confusion."

It followed from this that aside from limited public works expenditures, Roosevelt wanted a recovery program which would not
be a drain on governmental finances. Neither the Agricultural
Adjustment Administration nor the National Recovery Administration were. He had promised in the major farm speech of his

1932 campaign that his plan for agricultural relief would be self-financing; this was achieved through the processing tax on certain farm products. The NRA involved no governmental expenditures except for administration.

Both of these programs reflected not the progressivism of the first years of the century, but the means through which Progressives had regulated production during the first World War. This had meant regulation which would as far as possible protect both producers and consumers, both employers and employees. Here the parallel was direct. The rest of Roosevelt's program did not parallel the Progressives' wartime experience, for during the war, in terms of production regulation had meant channeling both factories and farms into the maximum output of what was needed to win the war. Now the problem in the thirties was one of reducing output in most areas rather than raising it, and of getting prices back up rather than trying to hold them down.

Certainly the nation badly needed this sort of a program in 1933. The products of the fields and mines and of highly competitive consumers' goods industries like textiles were being sold so cheaply that producers and their employees alike were close to starvation. The overproduction was also wasteful of natural resources. In an oilfield near Houston, one grocer advertised when 3.2 beer first became legal that he would exchange one bottle of beer for one barrel of oil. They were worth about the same. In other heavy industries like automobiles or farm machinery, production had been cut drastically while prices remained high. One need was to bring prices throughout industry and agriculture into a more equitable relationship with each other, and with the debt structure.

The NRA scheme in theory would help do this. Its antecedents were in the regulatory War Industries Board of the first World War, and indeed it was run by some of the same men. The War Industries Board had functioned through industrial committees; in the twenties these committees had evolved into self-regulatory trade associations. Unfortunately, as Roosevelt had found when he headed the association created to discipline one of the largest and most chaotic of industries, the American Construction Council, self-regulation without the force of law behind it, had a tendency to break down. When the depression had hit, some businessmen themselves had advocated the NRA scheme, but Hoover would have none of it. Roosevelt was receptive.

The theory was that committees in a few major fields like steel, textiles, bituminous coal and the like, would draw up codes of fair practice for the industry. These would not only stabilize the price structure, but also protect the wages and working conditions of labor. Even consumers would benefit, presumably through receiving more wages or profits, and thus enjoying larger purchasing power with which to buy goods at somewhat higher prices.

In practice, the NRA program went awry. Too many committees drew up too many codes embodying many sorts of unenforceable provisions. There was a code even for the mopstick industry. What was more important, some manufacturers rushed to turn out quantities of goods at the old wage and raw material level before the code went into effect, hoping then to sell these goods at new higher prices. Consequently during the summer of 1933 there was a short NRA boom when industrial production jumped to 101 per cent of the 1923–25 level, and wholesale prices rose from an index figure of 60.2 in March to 71.2 by October. The crop reduction program of the AAA led to a corresponding rise in agricultural prices.

Had consumers at the same time enjoyed a correspondingly higher purchasing power, the recovery scheme might well have worked. Some of its designers had visualized pouring the additional dollars into consumers' pockets through a heavy public works spending program. Indeed the bill which created the NRA also set up a Public Works Administration with $3,300,000,000 to spend. This money could have been poured here and there into the economy where it was most needed to "prime the pump." But Roosevelt and his most influential advisers did not want to give such an enormous spending power to the administrator of the NRA, nor had they really accepted the deficit spending school of thought. Hence while some of the money being spent by the New Deal went for immediate relief of one form or another, it went to people so close to starvation that they were forced to spend what they received on bare necessities. This was of little aid in priming the pump. The public works fund, which could have served that purpose, went to that sturdy old Progressive, "Honest Harold" Ickes. He slowly went about the process of allocating it in such

a way that the government and the public would get a return of
one hundred cents (or preferably more) on every dollar spent.
Raymond Moley has suggested that if only the cautious Ickes had
headed the NRA and the impetuous Johnson the Public Works
Administration the scheme might have worked.

Without a huge transfusion of dollars into the economy, the industrial and agricultural recovery programs sagged in the fall of
1933. Roosevelt turned to currency manipulation to try to get
prices up. He explained to a critical Congressman, "I have always favored sound money, and do now, but it is 'too darned sound'
when it takes so much of farm products to buy a dollar." Roosevelt also accepted a makeshift work relief program, the Civil Works
Administration, to carry the destitute through the winter.

Already the New Deal honeymoon was over, and in 1934 and
1935 a sharp political struggle between Roosevelt and the right
began to take form. To conservatives, Roosevelt was shattering
the constitution with his economic legislation. Al Smith was attacking the devaluated currency as "baloney dollars," and was
writing articles with such titles as "Is the Constitution Still There?"
and "Does the Star-Spangled Banner Still Wave?" Former President Hoover published his powerful jeremiad, *The Challenge to
Liberty*.

Many businessmen complained against the NRA restrictions,
the favoritism allegedly being shown to organized labor, and the
higher taxes. Although some of them had advocated the NRA,
the significant fact was that the thinking of most businessmen seems
to have remained about what it had been in the 1920's. They were
eager for aid from the government, as long as it involved no
obligations on their part or restrictions against them. They wanted
a government which could protect their domestic markets with a
high tariff wall, and at the same time seek out foreign markets for
them, a court system which could discipline organized labor with
injunctions, and a tax structure which (as under Secretary of the
Treasury Mellon) would take no enormous bite of large profits,
and yet retain disciplinary levies on the lower-middle income
groups. All these policies they could understand and condone. The
New Deal, which would confer other benefits upon them, but re-
quire corresponding obligations, they could not.

This hostile thinking which began to develop among the business community was sincere. Businessmen genuinely believed that under the New Deal program too large a share of their income had to go to organized labor, and too much to the government. They freely predicted federal bankruptcy as the deficit began to mount. If they had capital to commit, they refused to expend it on new plants and facilities (except for some introduction of labor-saving machinery). They were too unsure of the future, they complained, because they could not tell what that man in the White House might propose next. Business needed a "breathing spell," Roy Howard wrote Roosevelt, and the President promised one. Nevertheless, the legislative requests continued unabated.

All this, important though it is in delineating the ideology of businessmen, is not the whole story. The fact is that during the long bleak years after October 1929 they had slipped into a depression way of thinking. They regarded American industry as being over-built; they looked upon the American market as being permanently contracted. By 1937 when industrial production and stock dividends were up to within ten percent of the 1929 peak, capital expenditures continued to drag along the depression floor. Industrialists did not engage in the large-scale spending for expansion which has been a significant factor in the boom since 1945. As late as 1940 to 1941, many of them were loathe to take the large defense orders which required construction of new plants. Unquestionably the pessimism of businessmen during the thirties, whether or not linked to their hatred of Roosevelt and fear of the New Deal, was as significant a factor in perpetuating the depression, as their optimism since the war has been in perpetuating the boom.

The paradox is that some of the New Deal measures against which the businessmen fought helped introduce into the economy some of the stabilizers which today help give businessmen confidence in the continuation of prosperity. These came despite, not because of, the businessmen. Roosevelt long continued to try to co-operate with the leaders of industry and banking. Their anger toward him, and frequently-expressed statements that he had betrayed his class, at times bewildered and even upset him. For the most part he laughed them off. He hung in his bedroom a favorite cartoon. It showed a little girl at the door of a fine suburban home, apparently tattling to her mother, "Johnny wrote a dirty word on the sidewalk." And the word, of course, was "Roosevelt."

To some of his old friends who complained to him, he would reply with patience and humor. Forever he was trying to point out to them the human side of the problem of the depression. Perhaps the best illustration is a witty interchange with a famous doctor for whom he had deep affection. The doctor wired him in March 1935:

"Pediatricians have long been perplexed by difficulty of weaning infant from breast or bottle to teaspoon or cup. The shift often establishes permanent neurosis in subsequent adult. According to report in evening paper twenty-two million citizen infants now hang on federal breasts. Can you wean them doctor and prevent national neurosis?"

Roosevelt promptly replied:

"As a young interne you doubtless realize that the interesting transitional process, which you describe in your telegram, presupposes that the bottle, teaspoon, or cup is not empty. Such vehicles of feeding, if empty produce flatulence and the patient dies from a lack of nutrition.

"The next question on your examination paper is, therefore, the following:

"Assuming that the transitional period has arrived, where is the Doctor to get the food from to put in the new container?"

As time went on, and the attacks became virulent from some quarters, at times even passing the bounds of decency, Roosevelt struck back vigorously. During his campaign in 1936 he excoriated the "economic royalists." When he wound up the campaign in Madison Square Garden, he declared:

"We had to struggle with the old enemies of peace—business and financial monopoly, speculation, reckless banking, class antagonism, sectionalism, war profiteering. They had begun to consider the Government of the United States as a mere appendage to their own affairs. And we know now that Government by organized money is just as dangerous as Government by organized mob.

"Never before in all our history have these forces been so united against one candidate as they stand today. They are unanimous in their hate for me—and I welcome their hatred."

To these sharp words Roosevelt had come from his position early in the New Deal as the impartial arbiter of American economic forces. He had come to them less because of what he considered as betrayal from the right than through pressure from the left. How had this pressure applied between 1934 and the campaign of 1936?

Back in 1934, while the economic temperature chart of the near frozen depression victim had fluctuated up and down, still dangerously below normal, the dispossessed millions began to look at the New Deal with despair or even disillusion. Those workers going on strike to obtain the twenty-five or thirty-five cents an hour minimum wage or the collective bargaining privileges promised by the NRA began to wisecrack that NRA stood for the National Run-Around. Some of them and of the unemployed millions in northern cities still dependent upon meager relief handouts, began to listen to the stirring radio addresses of Father Charles Coughlin. Old people began to pay five cents a week dues to Dr. Francis Townsend's clubs, which promised them fantastically large benefits. Throughout the South (and even in parts of the North) the dispossessed small farmers listened with enthusiasm to the exhortations of the Louisiana Kingfish, Huey Long, that he would share the wealth to make every man a king.

Many Democratic politicians were surprisingly oblivious to these rumblings and mutterings. Much of the private conversation of men like Vice President John Nance Garner sounded like the public demands of the Liberty Leaguers: cut relief and balance the budget. Garner, who spent the 1934 campaign hunting and fishing in Texas, predicted the usual mid-term loss of a few congressional seats back to the Republicans. Instead the Democrats picked up a startling number of new seats in both houses of Congress. The dispossessed had continued to vote with the Democratic party—but perhaps because there was no alternative but the Republicans who offered only retrenchment. Charles Beard commented that the 1934 election was "thunder on the left."

President Roosevelt, who was brilliantly sensitive to political forces, sensed fully the threat from the left. At the beginning of that crisis year 1935 he proposed in his annual message to Congress the enactment of a program to reinforce "the security of the men, women, and children of the nation" in their livelihood, to protect them against the major hazards and vicissitudes of life, and to enable them to obtain decent homes. In this increased emphasis upon security and reform, Professor Basil Rauch sees the beginnings of a second New Deal.

Certainly the pattern as it emerged in the next year was a brilliant one. Roosevelt neutralized Huey Long with the "soak the rich" tax, the "holding company death sentence," and with various measures directly of benefit to the poorer farmers of the South. Before an assassin's bullet felled Long, his political strength was already undercut. Similarly Roosevelt undermined the Townsend movement by pressing passage of the Social Security Act, which provided at least small benefits for the aged, at the same time that a congressional investigation disclosed how men around Townsend were fattening themselves on the nickels of millions of the aged. As for Father Coughlin, the Treasury announced that money from his coffers had gone into silver speculation at a time he had been loudly advocating that the government buy more silver at higher prices. More important, Coughlin had less appeal to employed workers after the new National Labor Relations Act raised a benign federal umbrella over collective bargaining. For the unemployed, a huge and substantial work relief program, the Works Progress Administration, came into existence.

Partly all this involved incisive political counterthrusts; partly it was a program Roosevelt had favored anyway. In any event, combined with Roosevelt's direct and effective appeal in radio fireside chats, it caused the dispossessed to look to him rather than to demagogues as their champion. Millions of them or their relations received some direct aid from the New Deal, whether a small crop payment or a WPA check. Millions more received wage boosts for which they were more grateful to Roosevelt than to their employers. Others through New Deal mortgage legislation had held onto their farms or homes. All these people, benefitting directly or indirectly, looked to Roosevelt as the source of their improved economic condition, and they were ready to vote accordingly. Roosevelt, who had been nominated in 1932 as the candidate of the South and the West, the champion of the farmer and the middle-class "forgotten man," after 1936 became increasingly the leader of the urban masses and the beneficiary of the growing power of organized labor.

What happened seems sharper and clearer in retrospect than it did at the time. Secretary Ickes, recording repeatedly in his diary during the early months of 1935 that the President was losing his grip, was echoing what many New Dealers and part of the public felt. They did not see a sharp shift into a second New Deal, and that is understandable. Roosevelt ever since he had become president had been talking about reform and from time to time recommending reform measures to Congress. He seems to have thought at the outset in two categories, about immediate or short-range emergency recovery measures to bring about a quick economic upswing, and also in terms of long-range reform legislation to make a recurrence of the depression less likely. Some of these reform measures like TVA had been ready for immediate enactment; others, like a revision of banking legislation and the social security legislation, he had planned from the beginning but were several years in the making. Frances Perkins has vividly described in her memoirs the lengthy task she and her associates undertook of drafting and selling to Congress and the public what became the Social Security Act of 1935.

Then Roosevelt had to face the additional factor that the emergency legislation had not succeeded in bringing rapid recovery. He had to think in terms of more permanent legislation with which to aim toward the same objectives. That meant he ceased trying to save money with a temporary program of cheaper direct relief, and switched instead to work relief (in which he had always believed) to try to stop some of the moral and physical erosion of those unfortunates who had been without employment for years.

In part the Supreme Court forced the recasting of some of his legislation. It gave a mercy killing in effect to the rickety, unwieldy NRA code structure when it handed down the Schechter or "sick chicken" decision of May 1935. On the whole the NRA had been unworkable, but it had achieved some outstanding results—in abolishing child labor, in bringing some order in the chaotic bituminous coal industry, and the like. Roosevelt was furious with the court, since the decision threatened to undermine all New

Deal economic regulation. He charged that the justices were taking
a horse and buggy view of the economic powers of the government.
There followed six months later the court invalidation of the
Triple-A processing tax, which for the moment threw out of gear
the agricultural program.

The answer to these and similar Supreme Court decisions was
Roosevelt's bold onslaught against the court after he had been re-
elected in the great landslide of 1936. He had carried every state
but Maine and Vermont; he considered himself as having a great
mandate from the people to continue his program. Nor had he any
reason to doubt his ability to push a court reform program through
Congress, since the already bulging New Deal majorities had become still bigger. He was wrong; he failed. His failure came as
much as anything through a great tactical error. He disguised his
program as one to bring about a speedier handling of cases, when
he should have presented it frankly as a means of ending the court
obstruction of the New Deal. This obstruction was real. Many
corporations openly flaunted the National Labor Relations Act, for
example, they were so confident that the Supreme Court would in-
validate it.

However laudable the end, to many a well-educated member of
the middle class who had supported Roosevelt even through the
campaign of 1936, Roosevelt's resort to subterfuge smacked of the
devious ways of dictators. In 1937, Americans were all too aware of
the way in which Hitler and Mussolini had gained power. It was
not that any thinking man expected Roosevelt to follow their
example, but rather that many objected to any threat, real or potential, to the constitutional system including the separation of
powers. After Roosevelt, they argued, the potential dictator might
appear. It may be too that times had improved sufficiently since
March 1933 so that constitutional considerations could again over-
weigh economic exigencies. In any event, Roosevelt lost his battle—
and won his war.

While the struggle was rocking the nation, the justices began ex-
ercising the judicial self-restraint which one of their number, Harlan
F. Stone, had urged upon them the previous year. They surprised
the nation by upholding the constitutionality of the National
Labor Relations Act and the Social Security Act. In large part this

eliminated the necessity for the New Dealers to make any change in the personnel of the court, and thus helped contribute to Roosevelt's defeat in Congress. Further, the fight had helped bring into existence a conservative coalition in Congress which from this time on gave Roosevelt a rough ride. Many old-line Democratic congressmen now dared proclaim in public what they had previously whispered in private. All this added up to a spectacular setback for Roosevelt—so spectacular that it is easy to overlook the enormous and permanent changes that had come about.

In the next few years the Supreme Court in effect rewrote a large part of constitutional law. The federal and state governments were now able to engage in extensive economic regulation with little or no court restraint upon them. The limits upon regulation must be set for the most part by the legislative branch of the government, not the judiciary. Not only were the National Labor Relations Act and Social Security constitutional, but a bulging portfolio of other legislation.

These laws were not as spectacular as the measures of the Hundred Days, but in the bulk they were far more significant, for they brought about lasting changes in the economic role of the federal government. There was the continued subsidy to agriculture in order to maintain crop control—based upon soil conservation rather than a processing tax. There were all the agricultural relief measures which came to be centralized in the Farm Security Administration. Although that agency has disappeared, most of its functions have continued in one way or another. There was a beginning of slum clearance and public housing, and a continuation of TVA, held constitutional even before the court fight. There was a stiffening of securities regulation. There was a continuation of much that Roosevelt had considered beneficial in the NRA through a group of new laws usually referred to as the "little NRA." These perpetuated the coal and liquor codes, helped regulate oil production, tried to prevent wholesale price discriminations and legalized the establishment of "fair trade" prices by manufacturers. Most important of all, the Fair Labor Standards Act of 1937 set a national minimum of wages and maximum of hours of work, and prohibited the shipping in interstate commerce of goods made by child labor. These are lasting contributions of

the New Deal, either substantial laws in themselves or the seeds for
later legislation.

What then, is to be said of the recession and the anti-monopoly
program? A Keynesian point of view is that public works spending,
the other New Deal spending programs, and the payment of the
bonus to veterans of the first World War (over Roosevelt's veto,
incidentally), all these together had poured so such money into
the economy that they brought about a substantial degree of recovery, except in employment, by the spring of 1937. At this point
Roosevelt tried to balance the budget, especially by cutting public
works and work relief expenditures. The result was a sharp recession. Roosevelt was forced to resort to renewed pump-priming,
and in a few months the recession was over.

Even this recession experience did not convert Roosevelt to
Keynesianism. Keynes once called upon Roosevelt at the White
House and apparently tried to dazzle him with complex mathe-
matical talk. Each was disappointed in the other. In 1939, after the
recession when a protégé of Mrs. Roosevelt's proposed additional
welfare spending, Roosevelt replied by listing worthwhile projects
in which the government could usefully spend an additional five
billions a year. Then he pointed out that the deficit was already
three billions, which could not go on forever. How, he inquired,
could an eight billion dollar deficit be financed.

As for economists, many of them saw the answer in the enormous
spending power which would be unleashed if the government
poured out billions in time of depression. To most of them the
lesson from the recession was that the only way to right the economy
in time of upset was through spending.

As for businessmen, they could see in the recession only the
logical outcome of Roosevelt's iniquitous tinkering with the economy. They had been especially angered by the protection the
Wagner act had given to protective bargaining with the resulting
militant expansion of organized labor. Roosevelt reciprocated the
businessmen's feelings and blamed the recession upon their failure
to co-operate. To a considerable degree he went along with a powerful handful of Progressive Republicans and Western Democrats in
the Senate, like William E. Borah of Idaho and Joseph O'Mahoney
of Wyoming, in attacking corporate monopoly as the villain. There

are some indications, however, that the anti-monopoly program that he launched in the Department of Justice through the urbane Thurman Arnold was intended less to bust the trusts than to forestall too drastic legislation in the Congress. Roosevelt gave his strong backing to Arnold's anti-trust division only for the first year or two, and Arnold functioned for the most part through consent decrees. These in many instances allowed industries to function much as they had in the NRA days. The new program was in some respects more like a negative NRA than the antithesis of the NRA.

Thus from the beginning of the New Deal to the end, Roosevelt functioned with a fair degree of consistency. He heartily favored humanitarian welfare legislation and government policing of the economy, so long as these did not dangerously unbalance the budget. He preferred government co-operation with business to warfare with it.

Many of the New Dealers went far beyond Roosevelt in their views, and sometimes saw in his reluctance to support them, betrayal rather than a greater degree of conservatism. They had valid grievances some of the time when Roosevelt stuck to a middle course and seemed to them to be compromising away everything for which they thought he stood, in order to hold his motley political coalitions together. It is a serious moral question whether he compromised more than necessary, and whether at times he compromised his principles. It has been charged that his second four years in the White House represented a failure in political leadership.

In terms of gaining immediate political objectives, like the fiasco of the court fight, and the abortive "purge" in the 1938 primaries, this is undoubtedly true. In terms of the long-range New Deal program, I think the reverse is the case. These were years of piecemeal unspectacular consolidation of the earlier spectacular changes. It was many years before historians could say with certainty that these changes were permanent. By 1948 various public opinion samplings indicated that an overwhelming majority of those queried, even though Republican in voting habits, favored such things as social security and the TVA. The election of a Republican president in 1952 did not signify a popular repudiation of these

programs. In the years after 1952 they were accepted, and in some
instances even expanded, by the Republican administration. The
only serious debate over them concerned degree, in which the
Republicans were more cautious than the Democrats. The New
Deal changes have even come for the most part to be accepted by
the business community, although the United States Chamber of
Commerce now issues manifestoes against federal aid to education
with all the fervor it once directed against Roosevelt's proposals.
The fact is that the business community in part bases its plans for
the future upon some things that began as New Deal reforms. It
takes for granted such factors as the "built-in stabilizers" in the
social security system—something, incidentally, that Roosevelt
pointed out at the time the legislation went into effect.

In January 1939 Roosevelt, concerned about the threat of world
war, called a halt to his domestic reform program. What he said
then, concerning the world crisis of 1939, is remarkably applicable
to the United States more than two decades later:

"We have now passed the period of internal conflict in the
launching of our program of social reform. Our full energies may
now be released to invigorate the processes of recovery in order to
preserve our reforms, and to give every man and woman who wants
to work a real job at a living wage.

"But time is of paramount importance. The deadline of danger
from within and from without is not within our control. The hour-
glass may be in the hands of other nations. Our own hour-glass tells
us that we are off on a race to make democracy work, so that we may
be efficient in peace and therefore secure in national defense."

A SELECTED BIBLIOGRAPHY

Among the innumerable books on the New Deal domestic policies and President Roosevelt, the following are among the more
general and useful. Arthur Schlesinger, Jr.'s *Age of Roosevelt*,
taking a favorable, Keynesian view, promises to be the monu-
mental study. The first volume, *The Crisis of the Old Order*
(1957) covers the twenties, and the second, *The Coming of the
New Deal* (1959), 1933–34. Two brief surveys, especially suited
for secondary school use, are Dexter Perkins, *The New Age of*

Franklin Roosevelt (1957), and D. W. Brogan, *The Age of Franklin D. Roosevelt* (1950). E. E. Robinson, *The Roosevelt Leadership* (1955) is critical from a conservative constitutionalist viewpoint; it contains a 69-page annotated bibliography. In contrast, Mario Einaudi, *The Roosevelt Revolution* (1959) is sweepingly favorable. Among the biographies, J. M. Burns, *Roosevelt: The Lion and the Fox* (1956) is Keynesian, and critical of Roosevelt's leadership; R. G. Tugwell, *The Democratic Roosevelt* (1957) is excellent on Roosevelt's background; Frank Freidel, *Franklin D. Roosevelt* (1952–   ) is a multi-volume study. A vivid social history of the era is Dixon Wecter, *Age of the Great Depression* (1948); the standard economic history is Broadus Mitchell, *Depression Decade* (1947). Two notable diaries are those of Harold L. Ickes and Henry Morgenthau, Jr. The latter is the basis for the valuable J. M. Blum, *From the Morgenthau Diaries* (1959–   ). Among the most interesting and significant of the memoirs are those by Eleanor Roosevelt, Frances Perkins, Raymond Moley, and Samuel I. Rosenman. There is an extensive bibliography covering material published through 1950 in Oscar Handlin *et al., Harvard Guide to American History*. A lengthy bibliographical essay by Frank Freidel will appear in the *Thirty-First Yearbook of the National Council for the Social Studies*, to be published in 1961.